SIGNPOSTS OF MY LIFE

Elizabeth 'Joan' Hyams was born in 1930 in Dagenham and grew up in North and East London. A child evacuee of the Second World War, Joan was sent away to Theydon Bois and Wales during the Blitz.

A wife to Michael 'Murphy' Crumlish and a mother to four children; Michael 'Mick', Barry, Anne and Anthony 'Tony.' With eight grandchildren and three great grandchildren.

Joan is a well-liked and respected member of her community in Newham, East London and a regular face at Aunt Sally's Café in East Ham High Street.

SIGNPOSTS OF MY LIFE

Joan Crumlish

Copyright @ Joan Crumlish 2021
All rights reserved Worldwide.
Cover Art by Amazon Ltd

ISBN: 9798479185465

All rights reserved. This book may not be reproduced, in whole or in part, stored in a retrieval system, or transmitted in any form by any means (electronic, mechanical, photocopy, recording or otherwise) without the prior written permission of the Author, except for the purposes of reviews. The reviewer may quote brief passages for the review to be printed in a newspaper, magazine, or journal.

This book is a work of fiction. While reference might be made to actual historical events or existing locations, the names, characters, places and incidents are either the product of the author's imagination or are used fictitiously, and any resemblance to actual persons, living or dead, business establishments, events, or locales is entirely coincidental.

The author acknowledges the trademark status and trademark owners mentioned in this work of fiction.

In Memory of Anthony Matthew Crumlish
09.06.57 – 22.10.20

A hard worker with an infectious smile loved & missed by all who knew him.

The Wheels Inside My Head

They grind and grunt and give a lot of pain
The wheels inside my head are working again
I try to sit, relax and pretend there's nothing to do
But the wheels inside my head say 'get up you'

There's washing and ironing and sewing you know
Relax says my mind my brain says no
My body is tired my senses abound
But no peace from the wheels in my head I've found

The wheels go pounding I sit on a chair
I run my fingers through my hair
I take deep breaths and contemplate
But those wheels keep grinding wait oh wait

Don't torture my brain don't twist my mind
Let me relax some peace will I find
I wait and wait then suddenly
A great release washes over me
The realization comes to my brain
I'm free of those wheels I'm free from those chains

Lost Horizons

When young didn't you gaze at sun, sea and sand?
Imagine yourself in far off land
A king or master of all you survey
Now think forward to this day this here and now
You are not a king or master are you?
Or are you not a master of yourself
You have no far-off castles
Nor a beach to call your own
But for all that you can be a king to
Your own youngsters and when you see them play
There are your castles and your far-off lands
They are your jewels, your sun and sands
Your kingdom, your money, your evenings of pleasure
Your lost horizons are not gone for good
But passed to your children
As all riches should

Snow Use

I'm sitting alone and trying to think
My central heating is on the blink
It's cold outside. Ice and Snow on the ground.
The wind is blowing across our town.

I'm not grumbling though, I've food a plenty
More than I could afford when I was twenty.
I've lots of warm clothing and mustn't be sad.
But when the spring comes I will be glad.

You see I daren't venture out. I could slip
And at my age could lose my grip and break a bone or two.
Which really is not the thing to do.

So I'm sitting here and watching and waiting to see
When the ice and snow melt it will be good for me.

I'll dance up the street and click my heels
Like a seven-year-old – you know how that feels
Snows gone. No ruse. Snow use

Travel Manners 1

Why do people take large boxes on buses today?
Taxis and delivery vans are for parcels
and cases I say
Buses are merely people carriers
If I have a case I walk or taxi ride
Not get on a bus push and shove inside
When my four children were under 6 years old.
I walked them miles though, the pram could fold
My children did not kick up a fuss
Nor take a seat for which they paid to ride on a bus
Parents you are wrong to stand
Whilst children to sit. This ain't fairyland.
It's the world – it's real and no big deal
You do get yourself a bad press
Your example makes your young a mess
Manners they say a man doth make
Come on parents give your young a break

The Enemy (2011)

It does not wear a uniform
Nor does it carry a gun.
This awful thing. This illness.
It will invade my son.
But he is brave to face it.
His character is strong
He has been battling the enemy for so long.
He's had the chemotherapy
He's started radiotherapy too
I hope and pray
Each night and day that
'God is good to you.'
I hope you find a healthy path,
To tread, and ones that's sure.
A road to a clean bill of health
And even a road to a cure

Anthony

My youngest son is sixty?
Seems like only yesterday
He was a young energetic schoolboy
Going to the park to play
He was a swimming champion
He swam in Germany too
For several years an altar boy
And was chosen for St. Michael's big do.
To carry the Bishops mitre in procession
When he consecrated the church with a Blessing.
He served an apprenticeship for six years, became an electrician
And worked for his peers.
He married and it is for life.
He has two daughters and a lovely wife.
My youngest son is sixty!

A Wish For 2017

I want a miracle cure to come
Not just for Tony but for everyone
This curse this illness that we dread
Just seems to attack& spread& spread
It doesn't care if you're old or young
It invades the body of anyone
So, every waking moment I say a prayer
That someone will find a cure out there.

June (2020)

Dear Tony
The lockdown's made it hard for me
To get you a birthday card
So, here's one I made with pieces and bits
But with these circumstances
I hope it fits
Regardless of all I wish to say
I love you and hope you
Have a really happy birthday
God bless you
Love Mum

My Dear Son Tony

I take this opportunity to say
How much I love you
Day after day
I hope your birthday turns out fine
So, to celebrate and toast with wine.
Cheers
Love you loads,
Mum

Travel Manners 2

How pleasant to see a driver smile.
Pull into the kerb and wait
How nice when I say thank you
He answers that's alright mate
How nice to be offered a fare payers seat
When I ride free, people can be sweet
Then there are those that stand and glare
Because another is seated there.
When offered a seat among the ranks
They can't even be bothered to say thanks

Reborn

I owe no one anything, only myself
I am able to restore my own bad health
It's not me that's wrong, its life as it's been.
My Life must change as must life's scene.
A new path to be followed, new things to do.
New friends to make, new points of view.
It's off with the old life and on with the new

Timoshenko

Just a child in our house
Mum frightened by a mouse,
Tried to catch it with a trap
No good so dad got a cat.

Discussed names like Tom and such.
For our puss it didn't seem much.
News on the radio turned down low
Mentioned a Russian general Timoshenko.

'That's it!' I said 'That's his name!'
Timoshenko, he became.

I trained him to walk, to heel.
Tail held high proud and haughty I feel.
With 'come on Timo' along the street
He'd walk to heel close to my feet.

Got half my ration of butter and cheese.
I'd sit by the fire with him on my knees.
For years a part of my family.
Loved by all but especially me.

When adult walking home one day
Timo in the gutter lay
Hit by a car and left that way.

He'd gone. My furry friend, my general so smart,
Died in the gutter but lives on in my heart.

Timoshenko 1942-1948
At 12years old, Timo became a companion to me
I taught him to walk to heel, sit up and beg and I'd shared
my butter and cheese ration with him.
From a family of 9 to just 3, he filled a gap left when of 7
children I was the only one still at home.

Who Goes There?

The rain is falling in an endless stream.
I wake and think it must be a dream.
The gate is pushed open with a squeak, I start to giggle,
T'was meant as a shriek.
A cold sweat breaks out on my head,
And I lay shivering in my bed.
I want to move.
I'm stiff with fright.
A footstep on the doorstep, very light.
The door is pushed
Will it hold?
Who is it?
Who could be so bold?
Then a big grubby hand, through the letter box appears.
A click-a snap. The paper is here.

Rainbow

Colours so profuse
To copy there is no use
Nature paints a picture of desire
The pattern of every hue
Violet green and blue
Orange as in flames of fire
You wish to see a scene
Painted in that green and the colours of fruit
But nothing can compare
With its beauty so rare
Nothing will ever suit
Like a rainbow

A Scary Creature

Scary creature with bat wings
Scary creature will it sting
Face of angel so close by
And head of ape
My oh My A scary creature

Children's Poem

Come on kid's time for bed
Time to reset your weary head
Climb those stairs
Say your prayers
Did you clean your teeth and wash?
You do talk a load of tosh
Now let us quietly upstairs creep
Now I lay you down to sleep

Scary Creature

A child of nature some darkness some light
If I come face to face with him I'd get a fright
A being from the forest maybe just a dream
But the way he looks would make me scream
Is he a clown or is he a fairy?
Whatever it is, it's really scary

The Boggle Fairy

The boggle fairy waits for spring
Then works his magic conscientiously
To see that lambs are born and tulips
And daffodils brighten up the dark earth
The early promises of his strong
Imagination become real bringing us
Light after dark winter and giving him completion

Smile

Why so sad all the while
It doesn't cost more for you to smile
What is worrying you making you sad?
To see you smile would make me glad
So please cheer up do it for me
A smile costs nothing, it's absolutely free

Age

Oh well
My mind is young
My body's old
My blood is warm
My body's cold
I'm full of go and then it's gone
They say I'm old but they are wrong
Age they tell me and I find
Is just a stupid state of mind?
Till I try to run for a bus
My body then kicks up a fuss
Oh hell

Power

Why do you work such power over me?
Why can't you see I long to be free?
It's you can't wear this
You can't eat that
If you do it will make you fat
Can't you see you are moulding me?
Stifling me when I long to be free
To carry on and make mistakes
It's part of life for goodness
Sake

Skyscraper

Concrete mass pointing skyward
Ugly grotesque just a byword
Isolation of a nation
Skyscraper – good, no
It's an abomination

Underground

A long dark tunnel
Rats run around the place
A long dark tunnel
Hope I don't meet them face to face
It's musty and dusty
I feel I'm going to scream
I'm sweating and shaking
Then I wake it was only a dream

Feelings

To say I love you without words
Is so easy to do
To say I love you in so many ways
In ways that seem untrue
To put it in writing
To paint a picture of prose
Then give the writing to your loved one
So that he or she knows

Birds and Bees

Bird and bees sitting in trees
Nests high from pests
Hives all alive
Producers of honey
They don't need money

Balloons

They come in all colours, shapes or sizes
They grow and grow before your eyes
They're meant for birthdays and weddings
And to ride the skies

Dance

Dance, dance in a trance
Whirl, whirl with your girl
Spin, spin make her grin
Glide, glide side by side

Nature

Nature or nurture
Nurture or nature
Is it good or bad?
Nature or nurture
Nurture or nature
It can be happy or sad
A fallen tree
A humming bee
A butterfly floating around
Puppies and kittens, lamb's wool
For mittens
Flowers that bloom in the ground
Nature surrounds us
Nurture is found in us
But nature is all I have found

Home

Home is where I live
Home is where I give
It's warm and cozy
No one is nosey
Home is where I live

Time

She looked at her watch
It cost a dime
But it gave the right time
Tick tock tick tock
It was good as any clock

Beauty

The Sound of children's laughter
The smile on a person's face
The parent so proud as the child laughs aloud
Shames us who frown around the place
The beauty you see is just surface
You need to look around you know
Then perhaps you'll notice this beauty
And suddenly be filled with a glow

One Minute Poem

One minute
Ain't long is it?
You can take a breath
Or hear of a death
Or you can walk a little way
Draw a week's pay
In one minute
It ain't long is it?

The Library Visitor

She quietly sits
Tablet on her lap
Looks up and looks around
Then tap – tap – tap
She smiles now and then and
Tap-taps again
Mechanically communicates
Its company she lacks and awaits

These I Love

Bonfires
Breezes blowing
Leaves falling
Cheeks pink and glowing
Morning mists rise from the ground
An earthy smell all around
Autumn below and above
These I love

When you are gone

An empty plate
A vacant chair
A tossed-up bed
A vacant hall
A quiet air
The echo of the last word
My eyes are wet
My empty heart
The sinking feeling as we part
That's all that's left when you are gone

Retirement Time (1990)

I didn't always choose the way
That god had meant for me
I didn't always do the things
I should as now I see
Mistakes shine out like beacons
Now time has done its test
My only consolation is
I did my very best

Age of Steam

Railway dream
Train of steam

Down line
Station sign

Birds custard
Colman's mustard

Milk churn
Coal to burn

Fire lit
Move it

Train chuffing
Commuters puffing

Open windows
Flying cinders

Railway dream
Train of steam

None of these'll be on diesel

Pyramid Poem

Fly
The Sky
Won't even try
Just walk the walk
Shut up do not talk
Breathe in the free fresh air
Do not worry and forget all care
Live a lot love a lot and laughter
Living the dream and dreaming
Forever and ever after

Fruit Juice

Squeeze a lemon for juice
Squeeze an orange too
Mangoes Peaches Pears and such
Make a fruity goo
But the drink we cannot live without
Is Adams Ale
Or water to you

Smelly Feet

How could I tell him and be discreet?
He had grubby socks and smelly feet
A soapy soak and a change of dress
But his smelly feet made him a mess
Those things he had on the end of his legs
Made me want on my nose a peg
I really fancied him so
But with smelly feet
He'll have to go

The Green Man

His skin was the colour of leaves in spring
His eyes reflected everything
His roots went deep into the earth
Fertility from his time of birth
When winter comes he drops his seed
Which forms a place for his rebirth
Then from that seed another tree grows and
The leaves then form another green man
Who continue the cycle of the eternal plan?

Walls

Humpty Dumpty sat on a wall
Then the idiot had a fall
Walls are built to keep prisoners in
When they have been bad and committed a sin
Or walls can be built to keep strangers out
And for numerous other reasons there
Is no doubt

Seasons

A child is born
It is spring
All life begins
He reaches his teens
And as he grins
He grows to autumn and
Takes control
Then winter of life
The poor old soul
Four seasons – some happy
Some with strife
But four seasons tell the
Story of life

Loneliness

Being alone can be fun at times
But continually can be hell
You can be happy all alone
Or watch and wait for the
Telephone to ring or hear a
Friendly voice
Being alone and lonely -not my choice

Litter

Don't throw your chewing gum
On the floor
Wrap it in paper and what is more
Take it to the nearest bin and
Drop the offensive item in
Then our pavements will be clear
Of white spots of rubbish
Far or near

Food

Food means life
Without it we can't survive
Food nourishes body & mind
It matters not what food you've got
It's the stuff that helps keep you alive
Be you carnivore or vegetarian
Variety is nice
Your colour shape or nationality
Doesn't matter, foods a necessity

Joan

I was born in a recession, the last of Mums seven
There were 4 boys 2 girls and me.
So lucky was I to have love all around.
My big brothers and sisters kept my feet
On the ground.
With the outbreak of war
We walked out of the door just
Me and my brother jack
With a gasmask on our shoulder
And a label on our coats
We were marched to the railroad track.
The beginning of separation from all
My family and on arrival from jack
Not knowing when we'd come back

Noise

You give kids toys to silence their noise
Then hear bang bang from their gun
A car goes silently along then the hooters
Join the throng
Just when you think you'll have peace
Fireworks start and don't cease
But worst of all is the noise
That wakes you from a dream
Is the sound of panic shown by a scream!

The New Year Dance (1948)

My friend who lived next door
Was pacing across the floor
Trying to persuade me to dance.

She was without a care
I said I had nothing to wear
So, she loaned me her suit and I put it on.

We walked from home to the dance
I walked as in a trance
Not really in the mood to celebrate
But there with the help of fate
I met my lifelong mate.

We spent fifty-four years together
Then he was gone
He stayed by my side until the day he died.
He loved me with a love so true.
Our life together was great
He was my own soul mate,
And will be 'til I join him too.

My Journey

I pass this way but once but if I on life's journey find
A new and honest friend I must be kind
And give my care
To one whose journey puts them there
As on my way I go
Friends are not stepping stones
But bodies and souls
Brethren and kindred
So, I am told
Is it so wrong to love my fellow man?
I thought it was God's will
His vast eternal plan

Age (2004)

Oh well
My mind is young. My body's old
My blood is warm. My body's cold
I'm full of go and then it's gone.
They say I'm old but they are wrong
Age they tell me and I find
Is just a stupid state of mind
'Til I try to run to catch a bus.
My body then kicks up a fuss.
Oh hell

Easter

Easter Lili crown of thorns.
Christ died so man could reborn
On that cross or a hill
Mary shed tears as all mothers will
Spoken words hung head
'My God why have you forsaken me Jesus said
So, at this Holy time say a prayer or two
Perhaps say one for me and I'll say one for you
Peace be with you

Remembering Summer Things

Balmy nights, busy days
Trips on the river sometimes heat haze
Visit the seaside coach outings with friends
Picnics by bandstands walking in glens
 Swimming fishing barbecues too
Al-fresco meals are the thing to do
Long light nights, flowers skies blue
Then comes the chill autumns in view
But not to worry whilst walking around
Remembering warm nights when winters in town.

Death of Love (1979)

Wish on the moon and the stars are yours
Wish on the stars and the night is yours
But the night becomes long
And the stars no longer glow
The night is empty because love has died
Therefore, I wish the night to end
Or to be short as was your love for me
The brightest shortest day has become
The longest darkest night
Well may I wish on the moon for your love
But will love return to keep me
From the grave of my own sad soul

This was written when a young heartbroken man saddened by a broken love relationship asked why the girl he loved so much didn't love him anymore. All I could say was "who knows where love goes when it dies or why it dies." Happily, he recovered and married a very lovely girl

I Know the Good Guys Will Win

There is hope out there and I no longer despair
I know the good guys will win
The media play on the bad day by day
The muggings and slapping's and such
So, the readers like me only think what we see
Young people don't add up to much
Things I saw in one day made me happy and grin
Because now I know the good guys will win

Wish List

Given the chance I'd like to go to a place you probably know of
Called Arnhem.
My brother John with a parachute on was dropped in 1944
And became a prisoner of war, his capture by the Germans
Could seal his fate
His surname was Hyams and Jews were not a Germans mate
He got beaten quite severely which seemed so wrong
But being a beautiful tenor, he burst into song
And survived to live on

Virus

This awful virus came one day
And took those precious lives away
Places closed, streets become bare
The places we visited day by day
Were out of bounds and stop children's play

Surgeries closed when needs on hand
But NHS workers were grand
Isolation was the thing to do
Though some fools ignored that view
The idiot hadn't got a clue
Disregarding what's best for me and you

But we smile we wave and clap
We will with time escape this trap
To find after what we've had to bare
New friendships we made people actually care
When we then return to our run of the mill
We'll have lasting friendships
From times of ill

The Old Rag Man

The old rag and bone man calls on me.
He rings the bell each second Thursday
I open the door to hear him say.
"Mornin Lydy, anyfin fer me to day?"

He's old and thin but still an active man
His dog with him, its coat, black white and tan
Whenever I rummage, I sort out bits for him.
Because of his "Fankyew lydy" and his infectious grin.

He probably draws a pension
He's probably quite a card,
He's still got his independence,
For which he works so hard.

I'm pretty new around this district,
I'll help him when I can.
For the first caller to say 'hello'
Was the nice old rag and bone man.

These I Love Autumn (1971)

Bonfires
Breezes Blowing
Leaves Falling
Cheeks Pink and glowing
Morning mists rise from the ground.
An earthy smell all around.
Autumn below and above
These I love

When You Are Gone (1960)

An empty plate
A vacant chair
A tossed-up bed
A vacant hall
A quiet air
The echo of the last word said.
My eyes are wet
My empty heart
The sinking feeling as we part
That's all that's left when you are gone

The above was written by me when I'd said goodbye to my husband, who at the time was working away from home and had just left on Monday morning and would not return until Friday

Why?
(15th May 1972)

The three lettered word that says the most is why.
A child is naughty and the mother asks why?
Punished for a childish misdemeanour the child asks why?
The police are called to the scene of a crime and they ask why?
A person dies the family mourns and asks why?
Birds sing at dawn
Babies are born
Lights burn
Wheels turn;
But always someone somewhere asks why?
Why is the question that leads to another?
Yet it is never completely answered.
I wonder, why?

The Beauty

Her silhouette is slender
She dances with graceful ease
She bends and unbends without faltering
Flowing movements which are sure to please
With no covering she is lofty and aloof
When fully clothed she is perfection and youth
Why then do so many pass her beauty?
Why then do so many fail to see?
The tall willowy figure dancing or still
That beautiful graceful being
Nature's child
The willow tree

Autumn

She comes in with a mist in the morning
A warm sun and cool breezes abound
The leaves rustle and fall without warning
A red carpet upon the ground
The gardens are full of late flowers
Their smell of dark earth
Fallen leaves are collected and burnt
Or rot to form a bed for new birth
It smells of mist and mystery
Its bite tells of what is to come
It is mist it is falling leaves it is sun
It is warm it is cool it is autumn

Who Goes There? (1964)

The rain is falling in an endless stream.
I wake and think it must be a dream.
The gate is pushed open with a squeak,
I start to giggle, t'was meant as a shriek.

A cold sweat break out on my head,
As I lay shivering in my bed.
I want to move, I'm stiff with fright.
A footstep on the doorstep, very light.

The door is pushed. Will it hold?
Who is it? Who could be so bold?
Then a big grubby hand, through the letter- box appears.
A click- a snap. The paper is here.

Is it Easy to Love?

It is easy to love a beautiful creature.
Animal or human makes no difference.
It is easy to love a fluffy chick. Likewise, a pretty puppy.
The love of these things can quickly change.
True love as I see it is when.
A person is loved by another in spite of his deformity or abnormality.
The volunteers of the Simon community.
The Sisters of Nazareth.
The nurses and the friends of the mentally sick.
True love is when no reward is expected and none is given.
Men and women who give this love have found the greatest of God's gifts.
Is it easy to love?

Who? (May 1972)

Who is she that comes into my ordered life?
Why does she stand there turning me to Jelly?
Can she not see she is choking me with love?
What can I do but admit that I love her.
Is she aware of how I feel about her?
Without saying in so many words I love her.
Does she not see by everything I do and say?
She held out her hand to me.
She helped me when I fell down.
Her own hurt was hidden to be shared with none:
But in her lonely self her tears were shed.
The whole of my life was founded in guidance.
Yet never did she overstep the boundary of
interference.
What is good in me I owe to none but her?
What is bad is of my own doing.
You like I must wonder who she really is.
My father once must have felt the same,
And asked himself, 'Who is she?'

It is Not a Restaurant it's a Bus

It is not a restaurant it's a bus
I don't wish to make a fuss
But when I sit down in a nice clean dress
I have to be careful because of your mess.
You finish your burger or drop a chip
Some poor soul on this could slip
You hold on with fingers covered in grease
Its appalling bad manners I wish I could cease,
And as for empty cartons, cans and waste
To take them with you would show good taste.

If you can carry them when they are full.
When empty they should be no bother at all.

I don't wish to complain
But I say again
It is not a restaurant, it's a bus

The Beginning of the end
January (2008)

It's not important for me
It's not to be my choice.
It will come when the good Lord says.
I'll not need to raise my voice

We would all like our passing to be easy
We all want it to be pain free
But only the good lord can decide the time
Not you, not our relatives or me.

I've never known anyone could honestly say
At this time in this place it will be
So, I'll enjoy every day the good lord sends
Enjoy every minute until my end
Then journey with him & god bless me

SIGNPOSTS OF MY LIFE

Joan at Southend-on-Sea with her father.

Joan with her beloved husband, Mike.

SIGNPOSTS OF MY LIFE

Joan's passport photo circa 1960's.

Joan and two of her children, Anne and Tony.

Joan's Granddaughter's wedding at Gosfield House.

Rhyme Time (1964)

Dear bro. Bissett, I'm sorry to say,
Early this year we moved away.
The dances we attended with you as the leader
Are too far away we've left "Scarlett cedar".

The next time my husband and I take the floor
Will be at Ilford, with court sycamore.
So, no more letters to Tollington Park
Postage: - printing: - cost: - no lark.
So, bro Bissett, you understand clearly
Yours Mrs Crumlish, I mean yours sincerely

Recovery (2020)

After 4 months of lockdown
I went out so glad to be able to walkabout
Four blocks to get to my bank I stray
But to my old legs it seemed miles away
So, coming back without a fuss
I had to board a London bus
My heart was ready to go anywhere
But my legs let me done and didn't care
I must rebuild my strength again
So, my body won't ache and my legs won't complain

Winners?

Lottery,
Pottery,
What have we gottery
Not a jottery

I'm richer I've found
By saving my pound
52 pounds my dear
I could save every year

East Ham (2008)

Two rooms were mine,
34 Stairs to climb.
No hot water, bath, phone,
13 years wait for our first home.

From North London we came, husband, children and me.
Small terraced house, quiet road lined with trees,
Shops close by, post office too.
No supermarket or stores open late,
Shop owners' friendly banter, great.

Neighbours welcomed us, offered advice, leant tools,
For us beginners was like crown jewels.
Children attended local schools
Grew up made friends.
I grew up too, worked hard to blend.

Now East Ham has changed: shops gone I used to know,
People multinational, that's what the shops show.
We live in peace, everyone's my friend.
I love East Ham habitat,
Hope to live here to my end

My Valentine

Where am I on this Valentine's Day?
I know where you are
Far, far away
I speak to you everyday
You're gone and I have so much to say
Our lives were one
We breathed in tune
Then God called you home.
Far too soon.
New Year's Eve I was alone
And oh, so sad
That's the day we met and were so glad
Now February is here and lovers celebrate
Not us. No longer. It is too late
My arms are empty
My heart gives pain
Until God decides we should meet again
I treasure my memories
Each and every minute
My days I count long
But I will carry on
Until I reach my limit.

Darling I love you

My Window

I look through my window
And what do I see
An old man with a bicycle
As old as he

It's a relic of times past
With a basket to the fore
A butchers or bakers
Not used anymore

He walks the roundabout
The wrong way of course
Then assesses the kerb hurdle
Just like a jump horse

He's not elegantly dressed
Trousers, waistcoat and hat

He's got his way of working
I'll grant you that

But I look through my window
And what do I see
An old man with bicycle
Independent and free

I Look Through my Window

I look through my window
I don't mean to stare
But hooters are honking
A traffic jam there

It is dark street lights shining
Road blocked this way and that
No one willing to give way
Then starts a spat

Why don't you reverse?
Says an affable chap
You shove off: - tell him
You could slip in that gap

No, why don't you tell him?
Is it because he's a man?
Stupid woman can't see
The point of his plan

'Piss off, call the police,' was how she ended
And the affable man
Left the scene quite offended

After shouting and swearing and burning with heat
She reversed into the gap

Admitting defeat

While I looked through my window
To gaze at the sight
Traffic cleared and moved off
Peace restored to the night

I looked through my window
And felt a great pride
Because it all happened out there
And I was inside

Lost Love

You are gone
I try not to care
When I see that you are not there
But my heart sinks
And I pass on

Each day I awake
To the same lonely ache
But inside
I have died
And I pass on

I pray
Oh, how I pray
Every night and every day
For a sign or a word
From you

I relive every minute
Everyone with you in it
I smile
Though I'll be sad
Till I pass on

Wishing

How I wish and I wish Oh, how I wish my love was here

Do you think that I could love?
And hold him so dear

Oh, how I wish and I wish
Oh, how I wish my love was here
Do you think that if my love was here?
Do you think that my love would want me near?

Comes the day comes the day
Comes the day near
When my love and then my love
I'll have no fear

Many years I have loved thee
Many years will I love thee or
Comes the day of reckoning
I could not love thee more

Fund Raising

I'm having a do
Ladies bring purses with you
Men bring your wallets too
There'll be various Christmas bits
And sale of books
I'll get your cash by hook or crook
Donations are not obligatory
But you have to pay to be free
All jokes apart and from the heart
That day you I'd love to see

Poetry and What It Means To Me

Poetry is an expression of my feelings
If I feel sad, glad or mad
I write my feelings down it removes a frown
It restores a smile as wide as a mile
It eases pain or sorrow
It helps me live for tomorrow
It expresses my joy like a kid with a toy
It's a tool for my emotion and I use it with devotion

So Wise at Eight
(Clacton summer 1965)

While away on two weeks awaited holiday
A fight was started by eleven so called mods
Against two very drunk rockers, ton up bods
This vile encounter on the terrace that summer's night
Was witnessed by my children who took fright
Blood was spilled and bottles smashed
The rockers face was bruised and gashed

I put my children to bed it was late
Worried then my son aged 8 said
"Mum don't turn out the lights,
I'm praying for that rocker that his face will be alright."

With his wisdom he swept my fears away
I know now when he grows up he will be okay

If

If I were rich, a car I would buy
Around the world I'd sail or fly
No need to earn money, no need to try.
With a flourish, I'd sign this name of mine
Too a cheque, without where for or why

But- where would the pleasure be for me
With cash to be spent on an endless spree
Then I'd die and leave it to charity

If I were rich

Love

Love is a squeeze of the hand
Love is a look across the room that says all
Love is the warm body beside you in the bed
Love is "Thank you" for a well-cooked meal
Love is the anger when you turn up late but safe
Love is the smack and the kiss of a parent for an erring child
Love is wanting to leave but unable to go
Love is tears for the lost one at the graveside
Love is joy
Love is sadness
Love is pain
Love is forgive again
But Love is, I am sure

Corona Virus

The world as in biblical terms
Is suffering from a plague
We first heard of it spreading in China
But the information was vague
Then suddenly and swiftly

This dreaded lurgy spread
Leaving thousands sick and many people dead
Like in war time people sacrifice
Offers of help are freely given
Which is very nice
Maybe a lot of goodwill will
Surface and lift above this ill
We can but hope and pray
That it soon will fade away

Retirement

You've escaped
You're free
No more rushing for the train
You've escaped
You're free
No more answering phones again
Just relax
Take your ease
You can do just as you please
You can walk the dog
Visit the vet
Spend all day with your pet

You've escaped
You're free
Just like me

Reborn

I owe no one anything, only myself
I am able to restore my own bad health
It's not me that's wrong, its life as it's been
My life must change, as must life's scene
A new path to be followed
New things to do
New friends to make
New points of view
It's off with the old life and on with the new

Snows Prisoner (2013)

It's minute and white but I'll have you know
I'm being held prisoner by this thing called snow
It's holding me to ransom
This tiny fragile flake much smaller than a mouse
One flake alone is delicate and pretty
But many together could cut off a city
It blocks main roads and the railway
But skiers and tobogganists enjoy their play
I at 82 I'm a prisoner while it lays
Oh, please god of weather have the grace
To clear the snow from this cold place
So that I once more can get into the swing
Of life and be able to do my thing

Happiness Is? (1960's)

Happiness is
When Mr. Heath gives up his boat and goes by bus
When wage freezes apply to all
With no extra profits or rise too
The higher income groups
When each family including
The royal family, have one house
When popstars and film stars
Earn money in relation to what they do
When public funds are equal to public needs
This could be happiness;
But it could only happen in a dream
Therefore, is that what happiness is

False Smile (2014)

I wondered lonely as a cloud
That's floats on high o'er Hampstead Heath
When all at once down at my feet
I saw a set of glistening teeth

They were not mine and as I stare
I wonder who put them there
I looked around both north and south
To see if there was an empty mouth

No one to ask and no one to say nay
So, I smiled at the teeth and walked away
I wondered home from Hampstead Heath
And left on the ground that set of teeth

All I could think was no teeth to chew chuck
I'm afraid the owner could not chew just suck

England

Of all the place that I have been
Of all the places that I have seen
There is none as pleasant or varied or green as
England

Though our weather is sometimes like a fridge
Down across the Thames you see Tower Bridge
It stately charming and is forever England

When visitors come in their hoards to see
What is normal daily for you and me

It makes me proud and I am free in England

Aunt Sally's Café

There is a place I love to roam to
A place where I feel at home
To go for a snack or a meal
And get such a welcome I feel
Like part of Adam's family
Hello mummy he greets me
As do his colleagues and okay
He knows most customers by name
And welcomes us all exactly the same
Customers share tables when it's busy or not
Since going there, so many friends I've got
The place is called aunt Sally's its true
But it serves up a very big welcome to you

Age (2004)

Oh well
My mind is young. My body is old
My blood is warm my body is cold
I'm full of go and the it's gone
They say I am old but they are wrong
Age they tell me and I find
I just a stupid state of mind
Until I try to run to catch a bus
My body then kicks up a fuss

Oh hell

Bucket List

To go on the London eye
To view six counties from the sky
To re-trace my evacuation trail
Where strangers took in kids
Some were to fail
To visit Alicante to see
Where three relatives lay buried by a tree
And Ireland I really can't resist
See Giant's Causeway and Blarney stone to be kissed

Brexit

Will it be good or bad?
This thing named Brexit
The unity of Europe
And now we exit
We are a small island
Overcrowded overfilled
We need the support of these countries
Because of the best of wills
We can't grow enough food to feed us
We can't produce enough electric or gas
By leaving the common market
We are gonna be in a mess

Books

From the age of three
Books were life for me
I would carry one wherever I'd go
The library & I were in Harmony
I still love reading & so
I borrow and buy & as hard as I try
I just can't resist them you know
The classics are the best, they stand the test of time
The bible and Psalms, Thomas Hardy and rhymes
Help me through hard times
A book is a companion
Tis so.

Evacuation

A cardboard box with a gasmask in.
Kit bag on my back.
Nine years old, my brother ten,
We marched to the railway track.

We climbed on the train and there we stood
As we went on our way.
Not knowing if we'd been bad or good
As we left our families that September day.

We arrived in the village and marched in line
To the village church and school playground.
We then stood around against the wall
The children aged five to thirteen big and small.

The strangers examined us one by one
Like cattle in a sale
By this time, we were hungry and bemused.
Some young ones began to wail.

Siblings were separated,
Some only wanted boys
Some wanted children who could work,
Not playing with our toys.

I was lucky and unlucky in the people that chose me.
They were a newlywed couple but even they could not see
Being separated from my brother
Was very unlucky for me.

For a year he lived in the house next door.
I only saw him when at school.
As he was in higher class than me.
I didn't want to make him look fool.

My birthday came and so did his.
A day I thought we'd share
No such luck, I spent mine alone
Nobody seemed to care.

My foster carers were lovely folks
Who nurtured me so well.
Not so many of my friends
They had a living hell.

After a year away from home
We had to then go back,
To a new address our family home
Me and my brother Jack

No schools were open. My siblings called up.
All day alone at home, no place to go.
Then raids bombings, Ack ack guns in the street
Fires that set the skies aglow, shrapnel at my feet.

Dad visited Mum sister brother and me.
Went to South Wales and became evacuees
Again, a trek to the railway station
Another journey across our nation

In all five times I left my home
And went to pastures new.
New schools, new houses, another new bed
In one evacuation I slept in a garden shed.

No curtains at the window
No lino on the floor
Because of fumes from an oil lamp.
We slept with an open door.

Some people treated us like lepers.
Some were kindness itself.
What a culture shock it must have been.
For villages swamped with strangers
The likes of which they'd never seen.

The experiences I had
From 1939 to 1944
Did me no harm I'm glad to say
But it broadened my life much more.

Note: My first evacuation to Aunt Vera's and Uncle Bert's lasted one year but I kept in touch with them until Aunt Vera died and Uncle Bert moved away

My Street in Newham

When my family and I came here in the early sixties.
It was a quiet residential street an avenue of trees.
The road was really empty. The pavements were really clean.
Except for little deposits where doggie walkers had been.
All families were local but one dark skinned family
They were the ones that came to make friends with my family and me.

The docks were busy and buzzing.
Ship hooters could be heard. Boop, boop, boop.
On New Year's Eve they sounded and search lights looped the loop.
I took my youngest son to watch,
The last passenger ship leaves its dock.
Australian friends sailed on it
As it passed through the local lock.

Factories have closed down; the chemical works has gone.
Industry has changed or left.
People have moved or passed on.
But through all the changes good or bad I can say without doubt.
East Ham, Docklands, Newham. I love it and don't want to move out.

November 2006

Then and Now

When I was a child. trams were in Vogue
Trolley buses and buses filled our roads
Horse and cart was the way
Deliveries were made day by day
If a plane flew over in the sky
We all rushed out to watch it pass by
They were a rarity until the Second World War
Then are skies were filled with so many more
Street cries were usual like "knives to grind"
And Coal
To get customers was their goal

These are some of the things I miss
The whistling postman and the cockerel's crow
The children's playful laughter
The street singers singing soft and low
The one-man bends that children ran after
The corner shop where housewives and their like
Left shopping lists
To be delivered by a man on a bike

The emptying of meters by a gas man
Who returned a few coins where he can
We were all quite poor financially
But rich in contentment with our family
Sweets were treats we all shared

Eight toffees between four
And never did we grab them all or ask for more
We were content with so much less
We shared everything I must confess
We envied no one we felt so blessed
I listen now to the discontent
I see the abuse of cash badly spent
The see- want- have society of today
Shake my head in disbelief and dismay
When will we learn and undo todays mess
Remember patience and control and manage o

On so much less
Just like when I was a child

Swing East and Remembering

My friend Philip told me of a fun day
To be held in Crisp Street market on a Sunday
I got a 115 bus to poplar just to see
If there was something in it to suit me
Swing East was the name
I was glad I came

There were dancers & swingers dressed in style
Big dance bands that made me smile
There were retro stalls & food from the past
Like salt beef sandwiches & clothes which
Were made to last
But best for me was a hug you see
A surprise meeting with grand-daughter Ashley
The orchestra played strict tempo
With rock & jive & swing
The dancers were so nimble & didn't miss a thing
My feelings were of times past when things were
Made to last

These memories stopped me in my tracks
As one by one they came flooding back
1948 Tottenham Royal Hornsey Town Hall
The Round Tower Ballroom was the place to be
Where you met& made friends & started courtship
too

There I met my mate & the thing called fate stirred
Romance at the dance

So, all these thoughts went through my brain
Yes, swing East was great
Bringing memories back
I'd go again

Respect for None

On train or bus, I've no wish to see. A female passenger
Happily doing her make-up
It is a public vehicle not your bedroom or bath
Grimaces make you ugly and make me want to laugh.

I have no wish to observe your facial routine
It's too personal and should not be seen
This has not happened on three occasions I must admit
The last one at least didn't stand on the stairs
No – she decided to sit
Why do some inconvenience the many?
Manners – respect they haven't any.

What a bus is not
It's not a restaurant for meals to eat
It's not a beauty salon and please no feet on seats
Nor a parcel van for very large boxes
Nor a taxi for gigantic cases
Mums for three stops with bags and buggy you could walk
Put away that phone and don't annoy others with loud talk

Disrespect every day is shown these feelings I get and
I'm not alone
Come on people get on track let's get old fashioned
Manners and self-respect back
Just remember it's not all about you- but the travelling
Public are involved too.

Ode to DSS (1989)

Dear DSS I'm so confused
Like Queen Victoria I'm not amused,

Aged 14 I started work,
After 45 years I feel like a jerk

Fifty nice pence is what you'll pay
Now every dog must have its day

31st August at 60 I retire
With 59 pence I feel a desire

To scream or swear or throw a fit
This ruling government has treated me like manure

I'm feeling pained I'm feeling hurt
Oh, Margaret T we've been treated like dirt

Can you explain this lack of cash?
With 59p I won't get rash

I will get thin without a doubt
I won't get fed or even helped out

Not blaming you, I blame the system
Why people like me just seem to get hissed on

We are the tough thirties. The wartime generation
Who sacrificed all to save our nation

No, I'm not carping and I promise not to cry;
But PLEASE DSS. Please explain why

Note: I wrote this poem after being told what my pension forecast was, having worked for 46 years. The bumf and language used to explain to me was like a foreign language. I requested a response of words with one syllable. The response was four lines to say the forecast was correct (And not even in rhyme)

The Poetry Competition (2009)

A poetry competition
I'll win it without a doubt.
First of all, a decision
What to write about.

Could write about the weather
And what a mess it's been
Could write a social comment
Or a message for our queen

Perhaps that would be boring
And such a corny drag
Like stationers and newsagents
With top shelves dirty mags

I know, I'll write some good news
That seems a rare thing today.
I'll write about trains arriving on time
And planes that get you away

I'll write about things we all know
Like National Health Service and such
But on reflection perhaps I won't
It doesn't add up to much

So, I'll write a poem all about me
And how I was made to last
How hard I've worked. How honest I've been
But I'm a dinosaur and part of the past

So, I'll think about what to write
I'll think about what to say
O blow! I can't think of anything
So, I'll do it another day

Written as entry to Yours magazine poetry competition. A result of writer's block.

Who Am I

Daughter when born.
Sister too
Aunt and cousin to quite a few.
Wife for life
Mother of four.
Grandmother of eight that I adore.
Great gran to three
To many a friend
I hope they remember
When my life ends
We were all good friends

Central Park Café East Ham
(2010)

A most pleasant place is to be found
With trees and greenery all around.
The children's play space fills with laughter
I take a book and sit.
Then after reading quite a bit,
Refreshment is what I seek.
I walk into the café and am greeted with a smile.
Have a coffee and a snack
Which helps me get my energy back.
After being welcomed watered and fed
And my goodbyes and thank you been said
My footsteps take me home on the paths
That led me too Central Park

Acting My Age

Given up doing bakey
Should give up writing- that's very shaky
Not me at fault I know where the fault lies
It's the fault of the paper just not the same these days
Just like cups of tea when asked if I drink a lot
With- hands like these I spill most of it Clot
Same with shoes so narrow and neat can't get the ruddy things on my feet
Bras don't stretch so well round my back
Its elasticity that they lack
Mirrors lie when my eyes view me
Where's the eighteen-year-old I used to see
Who's that old dear who is looking out?
Someone I don't know – Me! It can't be
Still I suppose I shouldn't grumble
I can walk many a mile and there are so many
Things make me smile

There's skate boarders and lads with baggy-ass jeans
Girls with pierced bits everywhere to be seen
The fashion is to have a tattoo
If I get one done would it be 'wicked' or 'silly moo'
Growing old gracefully not so likely
Don't know how to so I'll just be me.

Age of Steam (1980)

(This poem has to be recited in the rhythm of a steam train)

Railway dream
Train of steam

Down line
Station sign

Birds' custard
Colman's mustard

Milk churn
Coal to burn

Fire lit
Move it

Train chuffing
Commuters puffing

Open windows
Flying cinders

Railway dream
Train of steam

None of these'll
Be on diesel

Note: Written in ten minutes after watching a TV programme about steam railways and restored trains, lines and platforms. The programme has conjured up the railway as I knew it in my childhood.

The Captain (1967)

We set off at a steady pace
No ripple could be seen.
And the ship she stalled a bit
Upon the foaming green.

Of a sudden the dark clouds came
Gusting winds tossed the foam.
Crashing waves broke o'er the bows
And the passengers wished they'd stayed home.

No sound was heard from the shipmates
Not even a worried sigh
For they knew that the man at the helm of
The craft
Was always known to stay dry.

The engines murmured the propeller roared
And the boat was able to start
They knew the captain would pull them through
With his calm and noble heart.

Her crew sat and waited with bated breath
The engineer bathed in sweat
Was heard to declare we've nothing to fear
He ain't lawst a vessel yet

The captain coaxed, cajoled and cursed.
They said a silent prayer
Oh God please help me to get them through
Then the weather started to clear.

AS the water calmed so his fear did too.
But no one was aware of the fright.
When his boat was tossed like a floating cork
On that worrying horrible night.

The passengers praised the crew.
The crew praised the man at the helm
He knew in himself who had saved them all
Was his maker in the heavenly realm?

Gypsy Flamenco

The gypsy music plays a throbbing vibrant tune.
They gather round the fire, in the light of the moon.
The stars are shining, the children barefoot play.
The swarthy males in neckerchiefs of every colour gay.

Their dusky women sit and talk, the girls, their body sway.
The dancers stamp their feet and dance till break of day.
What if the chickens they've roasted to eat were stolen and baked in the clay.
What if they were taken without by your leave- let not anyone say.
The twisting and twirling of gypsy girls whirling.
Will melt even hearts made of clay.

In the light of the fire, they can make man's desire.
Rise up and wash him away.
So, join in the dance and learn of romance.

By the fire in 'Romany way' stand up, arms high,
look up to the sky, twist and twirl around.
Snap your fingers clap your hands.
Stamp your feet on the ground.
Twist and turn, the rhythm gets faster

You're whirling and whirling around.
You get the beat, feel the fires heat and your feet fly over the ground.
You dance as you never did before.
The music stops, you beg for more.
A partner you've found, you dance as one, you hold her near, when the dancing is done.
You kiss her once, then you dance again, when the music stops, you know the pain,
Your gypsy has gone, to return never again.
And the gypsy camp moves on.
You return to the world, the run of the mill.

The music and dancing you once thought ill.
Will remain like the love in your heart and will –
Be forever after such a thrill.
Like the night you watched the fire on the hill.
And danced the Gypsy Flamenco

Shelter

There she sits behind her desk
Old before her time
Washed and brushed clean blouse and shoes
Showing the world that's she fine

She bright quite clever really
But without a place to sleep or play,
How can she be expected?
To sit and learn all day

You who sit in large houses
With spare rooms for guests and such
Can you honestly square your conscience?
When one room could mean so much.

To a child so very small and yet
So old before her time.
Can you really look her in the eyes?
That little child aged nine.

Shelter from a shower of rain.
To a stranger you'd freely give.
A home to a stray dog or cat
A place for them to live.

But what of these poor parents.
Who give give give and give

Separate those rooms, there for a week or so
Invite in neighbours' children then you'll get to know.

A bit of noise and fun.
House them on a short lease and when this has been done.
Get the cash and send it on – so you can help provide a place
Where these poor people can regain their pride
Finding laughter and hope
Again, the hope that once had died.

It Is Easy To love

It is easy to love a beautiful creature
Animal or human, makes no difference.
It is easy to love a fluffy chick.
Likewise, a pretty puppy.
The love of these things can quickly change.
True love as I see it is when
A person is loved by another in spite of his
deformity or abnormality.
The volunteers of the Simon community
The sisters of Nazareth
The nurses and friends of the mentally sick.
True Love is when no reward is expected and none
is given.
Men and women who give this love, have found the
greatest of God's gifts.
It is easy to love?

A Hymn for Him (1993)

In God we trust but not our fellow man.
Until that trust returns we never can
Live in peaceful easy harmony
In God we trust oh please God trust in me.

It matters not that Allah loves us all.
If those who praise him do things that appall.
Why can't we tolerate the difference side by side?
Then Allah will be happy just to guide

In Jesus name and John the Baptist too.
You read and wonder what it means to you.
Whatever you believe just understand
The church is us, Mankind the Promised Land.

In God we trust but not our fellow man
Until that trust returns we never can.
Live in a peaceful easy harmony In God We Trust
Oh, please God trust in me.

God's Will

I try to do God's will
I try to be a Christian
I try hard to be my mission
To help the fallen up
Forgive them their transgression
It isn't easy to do
When their spites taken out on you
I am no saint
Indeed, I ain't
But I try to do God's will

Poets

I'm sitting with a group of poets
Though some of them don't yet know it
It's good to feel part of a group
You feel that you could loop the loop
To put your thoughts on paper is good
In fact, my mind tells me I should
For my thoughts run around in my brain
All the time
And mostly they end up in rhyme

The Labour Savers

(English Literature Essay 24th February 1972)

He came in bearing the parcel like manna from heaven. Whatever could it be? He opened it.
Upon his face was a grin that threatened to explode into laughter. He produced an egg whisk and a potato peeler: not just an ordinary everyday potato peeler nor just the usual egg whisk.
The salesman had convinced him that it was extraordinary and no cook would be without it so bought it.

The egg whisk was two circular disks on a long handle. The idea was to separate an egg and put the white part into a glass then vigorously pump the handle up and down. That was the idea but what happened? Bits of shell were mixed with the egg white; splashes of sticky substance landed everywhere, the glass became wet and slipped off the table with a crash.

Nothing was going to dampen his enthusiasm so object no.2 was produced. The potato peeler looked like a piece of garden hose was attached to the tap, the water turned on and he proceeded to rub the spray nozzle over the

Potato in circular movements. Then the potato began to take on a furry look. The skin was gone all right but so was half the potato and approximately two gallons of water. By this time, he was looking a little dubious but he decided to try again. The tap was turned on full as he rubbed away with his fantastic peeler, suddenly the hose got a life its own. It kicked his hand away kicked in the air twice then shot cold water all over the floor, walls and operator.

By this time my poor man had become furious at being caught and making himself look a fool into the bargain.

We still have omelettes and potatoes it's true but now it is the knife and fork method.
Needless to say the gadgets have long been hidden or lost but they will never be forgotten.
When he is tempted to buy another gadget a mere whisper of potato peeler is enough to deter him.

SIGNPOSTS OF MY LIFE

Anthony, the youngest of my four children. A champion swimmer from age 6 years with East Ham swimming club.

Alter boy at Saint Michaels RC Church. He carried the Bishops Mitre as he consecrated the church.
When 15 he alone painted & decorated his Gran's 40-foot lounge perfectly.

He became my right-hand man & did all that needed done. I miss him & his most infections smile walk with God & RIP son.